Virtual Driving School Press

GW00863364

How To Pass Your

Driving Test

10 Simple Steps To Success

Phill Godridge BSc DSA ADI

www.DrivingTips.co.uk

www.VirtualDrivingSchool.co.uk

How To Pass Your Driving Test

Published by:

Mr. P. W. Godridge

Phill Godridge Driving School

156 Terry Road

Coventry

CV1 2BA

Contact details:

Phill Godridge

T: 02476 550087 / M: 07742 285090

phill@drivingtips.co.uk

ISBN-13: 978-1493712526

ISBN-10: 1493712527

Contents

Contents (cont.)

Introduction

Welcome. I'm Phill Godridge and I've been an approved driving instructor (ADI) since 1996. I started my career with one of the larger national driving schools and then branched out on my own once I knew what I was doing.

I decided to write this book as an alternative to www.VirtualDrivingSchool.co.uk, my membership website, and to help my own pupils during the time they are not in the car. Many pupils simply do not have access to a car for private practice but something as simple as watching an online video or reading through a workbook can keep them up to speed and help them learn the correct techniques quickly.

The rules and guidelines contained within these pages are exactly what I use every day when teaching. I found myself repeating the same scripts over and over again to different pupils, week in and week out.

I'd often wished I'd had some useful reference material and had tried using course planners and official text books, but I still found that I was making my own sketches and using my own phrases to clarify the information in the text books. I came to a point where I would go straight for my sketch book and leave the official book in the side compartment of my car door. I believe it is still there.

By putting together this book I'm able to use tried and tested material of my own design that my pupils seem to understand. Comments like, "why doesn't it say that in the other book", "that's obvious", and "Oh, I get it now", are the feedback I get, and I've done away with my mountain of scrap paper with hundreds of little sketches. Most things I need to teach a pupil to drive from scratch are right here in this book.

Further to that, I am sure that anyone using the information in these pages will learn to drive much more quickly than just with an instructor alone. How many times have you found something easier to master if the instructions were clear and you knew what you were supposed to do in advance? If you didn't have to sit for half an hour listening to an instructor explain how to do it, if you simply read the instructions beforehand and then put it into practice in the car, you could possibly reduce the amount of lessons needed by as much as a third!

If your instructor is worth the money you are paying, he/she will be pleased at your progress and will be happy to let you take the test earlier, after all, quicker passes give an instructor a better reputation.

You should use this book in conjunction with proper qualified instruction from a professional ADI. Knowing what to do in theory is no substitute for hands on practice. But knowing in advance what to do and how to do it, will save time, save a great deal of money and above all it will make life a lot easier for your instructor!

I hope you have fun learning how to drive and if you are shortly to take your driving test then I wish you the best of luck. But remember, if you can take care of the basics then there is nothing to stand in your way.

PLEASE NOTE:

Videos of all the lessons, with full talk through, are available at www.VirtualDrivingSchool.co.uk

Use coupon code **HTPYDT** to get **20% OFF**

Lesson 1: Car Controls

Assuming you have never been in a car before, at least not in the driving seat, you will need to familiarise yourself with all the Basic Controls of the Car:

The Accelerator, The Brake & The Clutch...

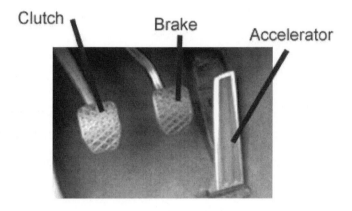

Squeezing the accelerator gives power to the engine and would make the car go faster, easing off the accelerator reduces the power to the engine and the car gently slows. The brakes make the wheels slow down and would eventually make the car stop. The harder you squeeze the brake pedal, the more effective the brakes become. The clutch simply disconnects the engine from the wheels and gearbox. With the clutch down, the engine is disconnected allowing you to stop the wheels or change gear. Raising the clutch connects the engine allowing you to pull away or enter a new gear.

The Handbrake & The Gearstick...

Gear Stick

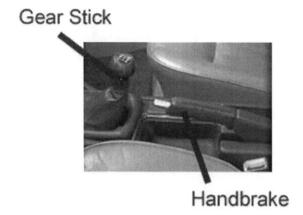

Handbrake

The handbrake should only be used when the car is stationary, not for stopping the car. Push in the button and lift until you feel resistance, the handbrake should then support itself and hold the car still. The gear stick allows you to change gear while driving. Once the clutch is down the gear stick can be moved. Do not attempt to move the gear stick without first pushing the clutch to the floor.

The Steering Wheel, The Dashboard, The Indicators, The Windscreen Wipers, The Headlights, etc., etc.

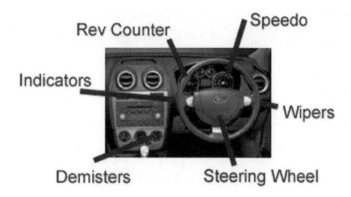

There are lots of different ways to steer a car... But only one way that will get you through a driving test. You must use the 'pull-push' technique, feeding the wheel between your hands. You must not cross your hands, 'rope-pull' or spin the wheel. Your instructor will hopefully go through all the other ancillary controls of the car with you; they vary from car to car.

But in the first lesson it is very important to actually get you driving. I don't want you sitting at the side of the road for an hour listening to your Driving Instructor 'banging on'. So I want to explain a lot of the basics right here.

In Lesson #1 you will be taught how to Pull-Away from the side of the road, then how to change up a gear or two and finally how to safely Park the car next to the kerb line.

First off however, when you first get into the car it is necessary to perform the 'Cock-Pit Drill'. This ensures that the car is set up properly for you to use and that nothing untoward will happen once you start the engine.

Cock-Pit Drill

1) Shut the door

This might sound obvious, but make sure your door and everyone else's doors are shut properly.

2) Adjust your seat

Move the seat backwards or forwards to suit so that you can push the clutch pedal to the floor without stretching or being cooped up.

3) Adjust your mirrors

Change the position of the rear view mirror and both door mirrors. As you have probably moved your seat, the angle of view from the mirrors will be different. You need to be able to see clearly behind you.

4) Fasten your seat-belt

Put your seat-belt on making sure not to twist it. You don't want it cutting into you if you need to stop suddenly.

5) Handbrake

Check that the handbrake is up and secure.

6) Neutral

Wiggle the gear stick to check that it is in neutral. Starting up in gear would cause the car to lurch forwards.

With the cock-pit drill complete, you are ready to start the engine. Turn the ignition key until the engine starts and then release. Your car will now be in 'Tick-Over' mode, this means the engine is running at its lowest safe revs - its idle speed.

Pulling Away

As you will notice as you read through this book, everything that needs to be done can be achieved by following a simple routine. There is nothing complicated about driving, especially when it is broken down into its simplest forms.

To pull away, I will assume that you have started the engine. So this routine is the same whether you are pulling away for the first time or from any position in the road through the course of normal driving. This could be from a junction, a pedestrian crossing, having had to wait in a traffic queue or just about any reason you've had to stop.

1) Preparation
> a) Push the clutch down
> b) Select 1st gear
> c) Apply a small amount of power with the accelerator
> d) Lift the clutch to find the 'bite point'

2) Observation
> a) Check the rear view mirror
> b) Check the right door mirror
> c) Check your 'blind spot' over your right shoulder

3) Manoeuvre
> a) Release the handbrake
> b) Give a right signal if it would benefit others
> c) **GENTLY** increase the power
> d) **GENTLY** ease up the clutch through the bite point

As the car begins to move away, use the steering wheel to guide you into a safe driving position - about 1m or 3ft from the kerb - and fully release the clutch once the car is in motion.

Releasing the clutch too early or quickly can cause the car to jump forwards or stall, depending on how much power had been applied. You could jump forwards or even wheel-spin if you have too much power, but stall if there is not enough power. Either way, you're on to a loser, so be careful to control the CLUTCH pedal for a smooth pull-away.

If you're pulling away up hill (A Hill Start) it's necessary to keep the handbrake on until you can actually feel the pull of the bite-point. Releasing the handbrake too early would result in the car rolling backwards. However, releasing the handbrake too late and allowing the car to struggle at the bite-point could easily result in a stall. Timing is everything.

A downhill start is a little easier. Simply release the handbrake and as the car begins to roll, bring up the clutch through the bite. On some steep hills it may even be possible to start in 2nd gear.

As the car pulls away and picks up speed, it will become necessary to change up through the gears. To understand this, it's important to know what the GEARS are doing and what they are there for.

Changing Gear

The most powerful gear in the box is 1st gear, not 5th as many of my pupils think. It is much harder to get a car moving in the first place than it is to keep it moving once it has some momentum. So as the speed increases and the momentum increases, the power of each gear gets less. 5th gear is a relatively weak gear; in fact as the car is travelling forwards at 50+ mph it takes very little effort on the engine's part to keep it in motion.

As a basic rule of thumb, I suggest giving the gears a speed range of about 10mph each. Thus 1st gear takes the car from a standing point up to 10mph, 2nd gear from 10 to 20mph, 3rd gear from 20 to 30mph, 4th gear from 30 to 50mph and 5th gear from 50mph upwards. These ranges are not set in stone; it depends on the car and the road conditions. Each speed range can be given + or - 5mph.

To change gear, follow this routine:

1) Push the clutch down and...

2) Release the accelerator - (at virtually the same time)

3) Change gear with the gear stick

4) GENTLY ease up the clutch through the bite point and...

5) GENTLY increase the power with the accelerator

Repeat the process for each gear change. It is necessary to be more gentle when changing through the lower gears as you are dealing with more power and therefore a more responsive car. Bringing the clutch up too quickly can cause the car to shoot forwards.

A good gear change should hardly be noticed through the movement of the car. No jumps, lurches, revving noises, juddering, etc. Aim for a silky smooth change every time.

Now... Before you set off in your car, it's quite important to know how the thing stops!

Parking / Stopping

To stop safely and in the right position is a fundamental skill that needs to be learnt quickly.

Naturally there's a simple routine to follow to accomplish this.

1) Mirrors   Check the rear view and left doors mirrors to see if you are being followed by another car.

2) Signal   Not always necessary, but if there are any other road users to see what you are doing then give a signal to the left.

3) Position   Move the car out of the driving line towards the kerb, by now you should have a parking position picked out. Aim for that.

4) Speed   Gently apply the brakes to reduce speed as you approach your chosen parking position.

5) Clutch   About a car length before your chosen parking position or when you get down to about 10mph, push the clutch pedal to the floor to disconnect the engine. You can now stop the car without stalling.

6) Stop   Gently control the brake to make the car come to a stop in your chosen parking position. Keep the clutch down whilst you do this.

7) Secure   Once you have come to a complete stop, secure the car by applying the handbrake and selecting neutral with the gear stick. You can then release both the clutch and the brake pedal. You have parked.

This same procedure is used whenever you need to stop, not just when parking. The positioning and/or signalling may be different, but the routine remains the same. When you master pulling away, changing gear and stopping, you are ready to deal with basic road junctions and get out in traffic.

Lesson 2: Basic Junctions

Having learnt how the car works and practised a little with pulling away and stopping, you can move on to dealing with Basic Junctions.

First up is the T-Junction or Give Way Junction. I'll firstly teach you the steps you need to perform a **Left Turn** both in to and out of a side-road. You will need to gain practical skills in speed management, judgement of speed and distance and as a result you will start to develop a sense of timing.

The Approach Routine

The surest way to pass a driving test is to drive around the test route without making any mistakes. Sounds easy when you say it, but in reality this can be extremely difficult. To help with this problem and to narrow down the vast amount of possible situations that you could meet on your driving test, I always teach my pupils to stick to the basics.

One of the most common road situations you are likely to encounter on a driving test is the junction, usually around 25 to 30 junctions on an average test route. If you can concentrate on each junction individually and make no mistakes, then a large proportion of your driving test will be taken care of.

There are of course many other situations you may have to deal with, but it is unlikely you will have to cope with more than one simple situation at a time. So, use one of the following routines for the situation you are faced with. When that is dealt with, you can move on to another situation.

A complete driving test is only a collection of these simple situations following on one after another. Take them one at a time, using a complete routine, and then if you should still fail... it would be down to bad luck, not bad judgment.

If you can follow this routine in the correct order as you approach every junction, and hazard, then you have given yourself the best possible chance of success.

The basic routine you need when approaching any junction is:-

1. MIRRORS

2. SIGNAL

3. POSITION

4. SPEED

5. LOOK / DECIDE

6. GEAR

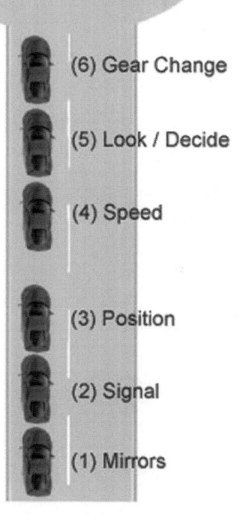

Approach To Any Junction

(6) Gear Change

(5) Look / Decide

(4) Speed

(3) Position

(2) Signal

(1) Mirrors

Left Emerge

Emerging means from a side road into a main road. The simplest example is the basic T-junction.

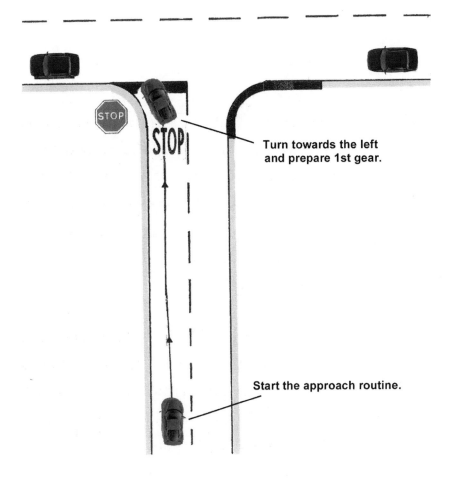

Turn towards the left
and prepare 1st gear.

Start the approach routine.

Other examples of emerging may be found at crossroads, but the approach would be the same. You could be turning onto a dual-carriageway, approaching a give-way line or a stop line, possibly a junction with no road markings at all.

The approach routine would still be the same.

1) Mirrors   Check the rear view mirror for following traffic and the left door mirror for clearance from the kerb.

2) Signal   Use the left indicator in good time

3) Position   Your position should be about 3 feet or 1m from the kerb. This should be the same as your normal driving position. As you approach the give-way line, you should turn to the left to follow the line of the kerb. Under-steer is a common error at this stage; if you came up too straight you would go wide around the corner.

4) Speed   Using the brake; reduce speed to allow you to stop at the give-way line if necessary. As the speed drops below 10mph push the clutch down to avoid a stall. With the clutch down, 1st gear can be prepared. DO NOT push the clutch down too early, this would be coasting.

Remember- BRAKES are for SLOWING, GEARS are for GOING!

5) Look   With the clutch down, 1st gear prepared, the wheels turned to the left and the speed around 5mph. You should look to the right and the left for any vehicles or other reasons to wait. IF IN DOUBT, HANG ABOUT!

6) Gear   a) If you decide to wait, stop the car just before the give-way line and then apply the handbrake.

b) If clear, the car can be driven away by lifting the clutch carefully through the bite in 1st gear.

NOTE: Look where you're going before driving away.

Be sure to recheck the rear-view mirror as soon as you have straightened up in the new road. NEW ROAD, NEW MIRROR.

Left Enter

Entering means turning into a side road. Again this can be seen at T-Junctions or crossroads.

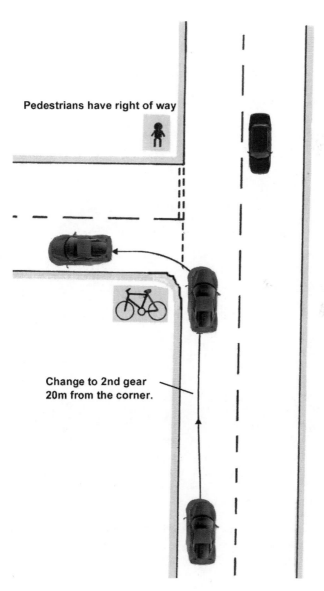

Pedestrians have right of way

Change to 2nd gear
20m from the corner.

These differ from emerges mainly by way of speed. It is usual to stop or virtually stop at when emerging whereas when entering, the driver tries to maintain a speed of 10 to 15mph through the junction where ever possible. It may still be necessary to stop and wait, but that is where observation comes in.

1) Mirrors   Rear view and left door mirror. This allows you to see the following vehicles and your clearance from the kerb.

2) Signal   Use the left indicator in good time

3) Position   Your position should be about 3ft or 1m from the kerb. This should be the same as your normal driving position.

4) Speed   Use the brake, slow down to about 15 to 20mph. On faster roads it may take longer to reach this speed, allow time.

Remember - BRAKES are for SLOWING, GEARS are for GOING!

5) Look   Check that there are no obstructions preventing you from turning into the side road, such as pedestrians crossing the road, cyclists or a queue of traffic . Assess the situation and make your decision, can you proceed or will you need to wait?

Remember, IF IN DOUBT, HANG ABOUT!

6) Gear   a) If you decide to go, change down to 2nd gear some 20 to 30 metres before the junction. Drive smoothly around the corner at 10 to 15mph.

b) If you decide to wait, continue to slow down towards the junction. About 10 metres from the junction push the clutch down and prepare 1st gear. Stop if necessary or proceed if the way is clear.

Be sure to recheck the rear-view mirror as soon as you have straightened up in the new road. NEW ROAD, NEW MIRROR.

Moving on... We now take a look at the **Right Turns** at T-Junctions. These are a little more complicated than left turns and include other subjects which also need to be covered. You will need to learn how to safely cross the path of oncoming cars and judge the width of gaps ahead between parked cars and oncoming cars. This is known as Meeting and Crossing.

You need to answer the simple question... "Is there enough room?"

Right Emerge

When emerging to the right, the most significant difference is the need to cross the path of other vehicles as you cross from one side of the road to the other. This takes more observation and, in most cases, patience.

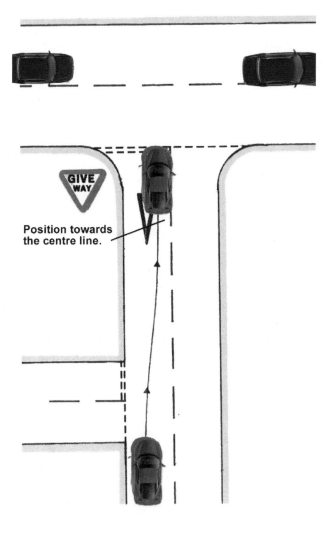

It is often less convenient to turn right, especially when crossing a dual-carriageway. However, the approach to the junction is just as simple.

1) Mirrors — Rear view and right door mirror. This allows you to see the following vehicles and also any passing traffic such as motorbikes on the right.

2) Signal — Use the right indicator in good time

3) Position — Move to the right of your lane, towards but not over the centre line. Care should be taken if parked vehicles can be seen on the right; you do not want to obstruct vehicles turning in.

4) Speed — Use the brake, reduce speed to allow you to stop at the give-way line if necessary. As the speed drops below 10mph push the clutch down to avoid a stall. With the clutch down, 1st gear can be prepared. DO NOT push the clutch down too early as that would be coasting.

Remember - BRAKES are for SLOWING, GEARS are for GOING!

5) Look — Check traffic from the left and then the right, there needs to be a bigger space from the left as you will be joining this traffic flow, you are merely crossing the path of vehicles from the right. Remember, IF IN DOUBT, HANG ABOUT!

6) Gear   a) If you decide to wait, stop the car just before the give-way line and then apply the handbrake.

b) If you have decided the way is clear, the car can be driven away by lifting the clutch carefully in 1st gear.

Be sure to recheck the rear-view mirror as soon as you have straightened up in the new road. NEW ROAD, NEW MIRROR.

Right Enter

The right enter is the first of the basic junctions where a real choice is needed. When emerging, the choice is normally to stop, when entering left the choice is normally to proceed in 2nd gear. But, when entering right the situation depends on the presence of oncoming vehicles. Anyone coming towards you has priority and you must give way to them. The chances of needing to wait are therefore 50 / 50.

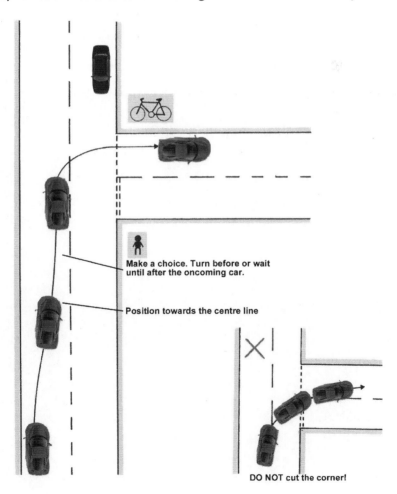

Make a choice. Turn before or wait until after the oncoming car.

Position towards the centre line

DO NOT cut the corner!

How To Pass Your Driving Test

Don't panic, just follow this routine:-

1) Mirrors   Rear view and right door mirror. This allows you to see the following vehicles and also any passing traffic such as motorbikes on the right.

2) Signal   Use the right indicator in good time

3) Position   Move to the right of your lane, towards but not over the centre line. Care should be taken if parked vehicles can be seen on the right; you do not want to obstruct oncoming vehicles

4) Speed   Use the brake, slow down to about 15 to 20mph. On faster roads it may take longer to reach this speed, allow time.

Remember - BRAKES are for SLOWING, GEARS are for GOING!

5) Look   Look well ahead in the road to see any oncoming vehicles, also check the side road to be sure it is clear. Assess the situation and make your decision.

Remember, IF IN DOUBT, HANG ABOUT!

6) Gear   a) If it's clear, change down to 2nd gear some 20 to 30 metres before the junction. Drive smoothly around the corner at 10 to 15mph.

b) If you decide to wait, continue to slow down towards the junction. About 10 metres from the junction push the clutch down and prepare 1st gear. If the way is now clear, you may proceed.

c) If you need to stop, be sure to do so in a convenient position so as not to overshoot the turn or obstruct traffic. Proceed with care when clear.

Be sure to recheck the rear-view mirror as soon as you have straightened up in the new road. NEW ROAD, NEW MIRROR.

Crossroads

To finish off the basic junctions, there is one more that needs to be mentioned. At crossroads, I have suggested that left and right turns are very similar to T-Junctions, with a little extra care and observation. However, it is also possible to follow the road ahead at cross-roads.

This calls for a slight variation to the routine, but not much:-

1) Mirrors   Check the rear view mirror for following traffic and the left door mirror for clearance from the kerb.

2) Signal   No signal is necessary as you are not turning.

3) Position   Your position should line you up about 3 feet or 1m from the kerb in the opposite road. This should be your normal driving position for the new road on the far side of the crossing. As you approach the give-way line, you should keep the car straight and square up to the line.

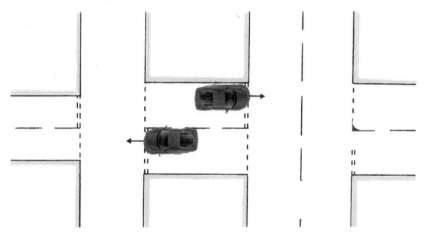

4) Speed   Use the brake, reduce speed to allow you to stop at the give-way line if necessary. As the speed drops below 10mph push the clutch down to avoid a stall. With the clutch down, 1st gear can be prepared.

Remember - BRAKES are for SLOWING, GEARS are for GOING!

5) Look   You should look to the right and the left for any vehicles or other reasons to wait. The space need not be too large as you are merely crossing the path of any vehicles. If you would walk across you should be able to drive across.

Remember, IF IN DOUBT, HANG ABOUT !

6) Gear   a) If you decide to wait, stop the car just before the give-way line and then apply the handbrake.

b) If you have decided the way is clear, the car can be driven away by lifting the clutch through the bite carefully in 1st gear. Look left and right as you cross the road.

Be sure to recheck the rear-view mirror as soon as you have entered the new road.

Remember - NEW ROAD, NEW MIRROR.

Priorities

As a final word on basic junctions, I'd like to explain how the priority structure works. You should refer to this each time you wonder who should go first.

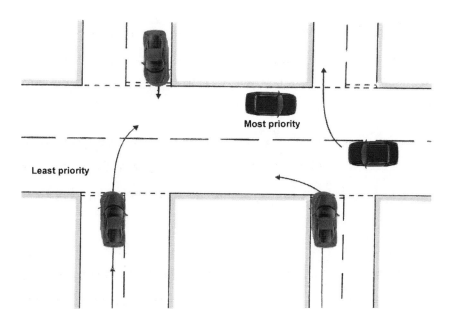

At the top of the list, with most priority are the cars driving along the through road who might want to turn left into a side-road. They have no other vehicles to give way to although as with any situation, pedestrians have right of way.

Next on the list are the cars on the through road who want to turn right into a side-road. They need to give way to oncoming vehicles only, not to anyone emerging from the side-road.

Next up are the cars emerging from the side-road, crossing a give-way line, and wanting to turn left onto the through road. They need to give way to cars on the through road approaching from the right but not necessarily the left. It depends how wide the road is.

Then we get to the cars emerging from the side road, following the road ahead at the crossroads. Naturally they need to wait until the through road is clear in both directions.

Finally, and at the bottom of the list, are the cars waiting to turn right from the side road into the through road. They must wait for all the cars on the through road and also any cars emerging from the opposite side of the crossroads.

If there are two drivers waiting to turn right from opposite side-roads, they will have to work it out between them. Get a bit of eye contact and decide who is going to go first. Usually, but not always, the driver who has been waiting the longest will go first.

Lesson 3: Roundabouts

I can see the look of horror on your face all ready. If I had a pound for every time I've heard the words, "I can't do roundabouts", I could retire. They appear to be quicker than other junctions, especially when there is a lot of traffic flowing. But that is the key word, flowing. Traffic moves quite easily around roundabouts because they work rather well.

As with all road systems though, if you put too much traffic through, it clogs up. But for medium density traffic they have a good design.

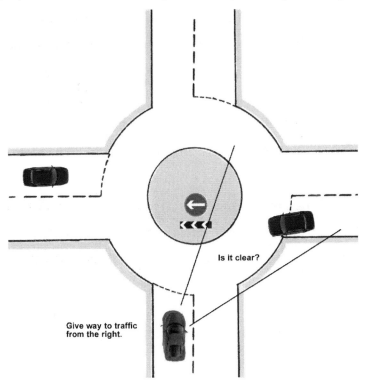

Is it clear?

Give way to traffic from the right.

Let me explain how they work - in theory. Imagine the roundabout as a clock face, you approach from 6:00 and straight ahead is 12:00. Any exit located past 12:00 in a clockwise direction, is officially a right turn. Only the first exit will be classed as the left turn. Other exits will be called, 'the 2nd exit', or 'the 3rd exit', etc.

All the traffic moves around clockwise so you will always need to turn to the left to get onto the roundabout. The final destination will only depend on the exit you take to leave the junction. This makes observation much easier, as the only vehicles that concern you will be approaching from your right.

Roundabouts tend to be more open than other junctions, less buildings and parked cars, so as a result you will often be able to decide whether to proceed from farther away. In turn this may allow you to continue at a slightly higher speed than for other junctions. Where there are multiple lanes and so more space, it may even be possible to comfortably drive in 3rd gear at around 20-25mph.

See the later section on dual-carriageways for help with multiple lane roundabouts; this section is only concerned with single lane or urban roundabouts. Use these routines for mini roundabouts as well.

Approaching a Roundabout

When your instructor or examiner asks you to turn to the left at the next roundabout, it is generally implied that they want you to take the first exit. Any other direction would normally be followed by the exit number, e.g. Follow the road ahead, it will be the 2nd exit.

Notice how similar this routine is to any other basic junction, are you seeing a pattern yet?

1) Mirrors   Rear view and left door mirror. This allows you to see the following vehicles and your clearance from the kerb.

2) Signal   Left for left - Right for right - otherwise no signal.

3) Position   On a single lane roundabout, drive in the centre of the lane, this gives you clearance from the kerbs on both sides of the car. Regardless of your final destination, you must curve to the left as you get closer to the line, simply keep the same relative position from the kerb.

4) Speed   Slow down to about 20mph, slightly faster than other junctions. The actual speed will depend on the size of the roundabout and whether your approach is clear. Slower than 20mph if necessary.

5) Look   Look to the right as you approach, look for cars coming towards the roundabout from that direction, and for cars coming around the roundabout towards you. Ideally you will see a large enough space to drive into, if not you can wait to see a space behind an oncoming vehicle, and then follow it onto the roundabout.

Remember - IF IN DOUBT, HANG ABOUT !

6) Gear   a) If you decide to go, change down to 2nd gear some 20 to 30 metres before the junction. Drive smoothly onto the roundabout at around 15mph.

        b) If you decide to wait, continue to slow down towards the junction. About 10 metres from the junction push the clutch down and prepare 1st gear. Stop if necessary or proceed if the way is clear.

What you do on the roundabout depends on the direction you intended to go, but your approach to the roundabout should be consistent.

Positioning to Turn Left

The left turn at a roundabout is going to be the first exit from that roundabout. Only the first exit requires a left signal as you approach. Once on the roundabout, continue to signal to the left and follow the natural line of the kerb. Leave the roundabout by the first exit and cancel the left signal.

Be sure to recheck the rear-view mirror as soon as you have straightened up in the new road. NEW ROAD, NEW MIRROR.

Positioning to Follow The Road Ahead

Ahead at a roundabout means any exit after the first one that is not a right turn. It could be the 2nd or 3rd exit, but not past 12:00 on the clock face.

Once on the roundabout, stay in the centre of the lane and follow the natural line of the road. As you pass the exit just before the one you want, check the mirrors (rear-view and left door), give a clear signal to the left and take the next exit.

Be sure to recheck the rear-view mirror as soon as you have straightened up in the new road. NEW ROAD, NEW MIRROR.

Positioning to Turn Right

The right turn is the trickiest to cope with because of the extra steering involved in getting all the way around the island. Other than that there is very little difference as you will see.

Once on the roundabout, continue to signal to the right and stay in the centre of the lane, follow the natural line of the road. As you pass the exit just before the one you want, check the mirrors (rear-view and left door), give a clear signal to the left and take the next exit.

Be sure to recheck the rear-view mirror as soon as you have straightened up in the new road.

Remember - NEW ROAD, NEW MIRROR.

Lesson 4: Traffic Lights

You can at this stage drive comfortably around the housing estate, but it's time to branch out. You now need to learn how to deal with basic Traffic Lights. Most estates have these junctions nearby, so there won't be the need to travel too far yet. The point is... once you have covered T-Junctions, Crossroads, Roundabouts and Traffic Lights, you will have learnt ALL the Basic Junctions.

Traffic lights are usually found at T-Junctions or crossroads that are too busy or possibly too large for traffic to flow successfully without help. In fact the lights make a difficult or even dangerous junction, easy and safe.

Before I go through the approach routine I want to make sure that you know the sequence of the lights. The lights come on in the following order:-

Green --> Amber --> Red --> Red & Amber --> Green

You may have seen this every day but never even noticed. I am amazed at the amount of pupils I teach who have no idea what order the lights work in.

Just to make doubly sure, this is what the different colours mean to you as a driver.

Green   Proceed only if the way is clear.

Amber   Stop if safe to do so, but continue if it would be too dangerous to stop.

Red   Stop and wait.

Red & Amber   Prepare to go, but do not move until the light changes to green.

Observation as you approach traffic lights is naturally very important, you not only need to know what other road users are doing, but you need to see the colour of the lights and be able to anticipate the colour they will be when you get there.

This takes some practice, but if you are always prepared and alert, then anticipation is possible and traffic light junctions become some of the easiest junctions to deal with.

Traffic Lights - Ahead

Traffic light junctions need to be approached in one of two different ways; this depends on the colour of the light showing as you approach.

First of all, let me explain how to approach a **GREEN** light. Remember the light is green now, but this does not mean you will be able to go, things change!

1) Mirrors Rear view mirror. This allows you to see the following vehicles, their relative speed and distance behind you.

2) Signal No signal necessary as you are not turning.

3) Position Normal driving position should be taken, about a metre from the kerb. If multiple lanes are present, then the left hand lane is normally taken unless road markings specifically tell you to use a different lane.

4) Speed Ease off. This means simply ease off the pressure on the accelerator, you don't want to over-react by using the brake at this stage. After all you are looking at a green light. This could all change, however, in the next few seconds.

5) Look Keep an eye on the lights as you approach, they may change. Be prepared to use the brake and slow down if the lights change. If you get to within two car lengths of the junction and the light is still green, carry on. This is known as the "Point of No Return".

6) Gear   a) If you can simply carry on then no gear change should be required, just reapply pressure to the accelerator.

b) If you have needed to stop, prepare 1st gear ready for the next green light. Apply the hand-brake whilst waiting at the lights. If you are waiting in a queue, make sure you can see the back tyres of the car in front. If you can't, you're too close.

If the lights change just as you arrive at the junction, don't panic and carry on. This is what I call The Mastermind Rule - I've Started, So I'll Finish!!

Be sure to recheck the rear-view mirror as soon as you have straightened up in the new road. NEW ROAD, NEW MIRROR.

In the situation where the traffic light is showing RED when you approach, it is just as important to make no assumptions about the need to stop. Again, things change, as you get closer the lights may change or they may not. This is where anticipation comes in again.

Follow this very similar routine:-

1) Mirrors   Rear view mirror. This allows you to see the following vehicles, their relative speed and distance behind you.

2) Signal   No signal necessary as you are not turning.

3) Position   Normal driving position should be taken, about a metre from the kerb. If multiple lanes are present, then the left hand lane is normally taken unless road markings specifically tell you to use a different lane.

4) Speed   Slow down gently using the brake, but cover the clutch pedal in case a gear change is needed. Deceleration should be similar to the approach to a T-Junction as you may need to stop at the line or behind another car.

5) Look   Keep an eye on the lights as you approach, they may change. Be prepared to change gear and carry on if the lights change. Be prepared to stop if they don't.

6) Gear   a) If the lights do change as you approach, you must check your speed and pick the appropriate gear. Usually 3rd for 20+ mph, 2nd if under 20mph and 1st when under 10mph.

                  b) If you have needed to stop, prepare 1st gear ready for the next green light. Apply the hand-brake whilst waiting at the lights. If in a queue, remember be able to see tyres on tarmac.

Be sure to recheck the rear-view mirror as soon as you have entered the new road. NEW ROAD, NEW MIRROR.

Also remember - Anticipate, don't Assume. The word ASSUME makes an ASS of U and ME !!

Traffic Lights - Left

Some of my pupils have more difficulty with traffic lights when a turn is also involved, others find it easier because of the reduced speed. However, both agree that left turns at lights are relatively easy when the routine is followed. This routine is very similar to a left enter routine, but there can still be no assumptions made until the car is relatively close to the junction.

1) Mirrors   Rear view and left door mirror. This allows you to see the following vehicles and your clearance from the kerb.

2) Signal   Use the left indicator in good time

3) Position   Your position should be about 3ft or 1m from the kerb. This should be the same as your normal driving position. Where there are lanes, you will invariably need to be in the left hand lane.

4) Speed   Use the brake, slow down to about 15 to 20mph. On faster roads it may take longer to reach this speed, allow time.

Remember - BRAKES are for SLOWING, GEARS are for GOING!

5) Look   Keep a watch of the traffic lights. If the lights have been on green, be prepared to stop if they change and if the lights have been on red, be prepared to continue if they turn green. As you will be reducing speed toward the junction, there is a greater chance of the lights changing.

6) Gear   a) If you get within 20 metres of the junction and the lights are green, change to 2nd gear and drive smoothly around the corner. If the lights change just as you do this, carry on past the "Point of No Return".

                  b) If the light remains red or has changed to red before the 20 metre mark, prepare 1st gear as you stop the car. Secure the hand-brake if you need to wait. If in a queue, see tyres on tarmac.

Be sure to recheck the rear-view mirror as soon as you have straightened up in the new road. NEW ROAD, NEW MIRROR.

Traffic Lights - Right

The right turn at traffic lights can send many pupils into a blind panic. It is the thought of waiting in the middle of a large junction, with lots of cars coming from every direction, followed by the fear of stalling just at the wrong moment.

These thoughts are common and perfectly normal, but this breaks Golden Rule #1: DON'T PANIC. You need a routine to follow, step by step. When you concentrate on a routine you don't panic, simple.

Wait here until it's clear to go.

The "Nearside-To-Nearside" technique used at most traffic light junctions

How To Pass Your Driving Test

Use this routine:-

1) Mirrors   Rear view and right door mirror. This allows you to see the following vehicles and also any passing traffic in the right hand lane.

2) Signal   Use the right indicator in good time

3) Position   Move to the right of your lane, or change to the right hand lane where multiple lanes exist.

4) Speed   Use the brake, slow down to about 15mph, it will be unusual to carry on at this junction especially at busy times.

5) Look   Check the lights as you approach and be prepared for a change. It is also important to watch the oncoming traffic as you have to deal with them next. Don't worry, by now you are only travelling slowly, this gives you plenty of time to decide.

6) Gear   a) If the light stays green and there are no obstructions, you can change to 2nd gear and drive smoothly around the corner at 10 to 15mph.

b) If you need to wait in the 'centre', prepare 1st gear

as you stop. For 'centre', adopt either the near-side to near-side position (pictured) or the offside to offside position where the two cars would drive past each other before turning.

c) After waiting at a red light, be patient. There will usually be a queue waiting to move. Crawl forward on clutch control to the 'centre' and wait.

You will have two or possibly three opportunities to proceed:-

- **Firstly** there may be a gap in the traffic.

- **Secondly** the lights may change while you wait. Make sure the oncoming cars are actually stopping before you go. Use the Mastermind Rule – "I've started so I'll finish."

- **Thirdly** there may be a filter light. If a green arrow lights up pointing to the right, then the oncoming cars will have a red light and it should be safe for you to go.

Use **Golden Rule #3 - Take Your Time** and always remember New Road, New Mirror.

Lesson 5: Hazards

Now you know how to drive around all the basic junctions there's no stopping you. You can get out of your local area and start to explore the city. As you venture out onto the Main Roads you will cope with Bigger, Busier Roads and Junctions.

You will learn all about Pedestrian Crossings, Road Markings, Traffic Signs and Driver Behaviour.

This is the stage where You Really Start Learning To Drive.

Let's deal now with arguably the most important skill for safe driving on the open road - Hazard Perception. A hazard is defined as any condition which may cause you to change course or speed.

Naturally a junction falls into this category but they have their own routines, in this case I'm referring to hazards such as; parked cars, pedestrian crossings, children, dogs, road works, bends / curves, hills and bridges, puddles, loose road surface, and anything you may encounter whilst driving that may cause you to have to change the course or the speed of the car in order to proceed safely.

The Hazard Routine

The most basic hazard routine to follow is simply:-

Mirror   Check the rear view mirror having seen the hazard ahead.

Speed   Ease off the accelerator to allow you some thinking time.

Look   Identify the type of hazard facing you and look well ahead to get the best view.

Assess   What is the safest course of action? Have you dealt with this situation before?

Decide   The decision is usually between go or wait. Black and white in most cases.

Action   Having decided what to do, take action to deal with the hazard. Be positive.

Examples:-

1) Passing parked cars:

Mirror   Check behind for following vehicles.

Speed   Ease off to give more thinking time.

Look   Check well ahead for oncoming cars. Look for other possible hazards.

Assess   whether or not it is safe to overtake.

Decide   to overtake or hold back.

Action   Change gear if necessary, signal if necessary, proceed when safe giving a metre clearance to the parked car.

2) Pedestrian Crossings:

There are in fact FIVE different types of pedestrian crossing, not including those manned by a police officer or school crossing patrol.

A Zebra Crossing can be identified by the black and white stripes across the road and the flashing beacons at either end. Pedestrians have absolute right of way on these crossings, 24 hours a day. If you see a pedestrian waiting to cross, you MUST stop and wait.

A Pelican Crossing is a traffic light controlled crossing. Pelican stands for **PE**destrian **LI**ght **CON**trol (sort of!). The pedestrian pushes the button and must wait for the lights to change. The driver only needs to wait if the lights are red. The flashing amber light tells the driver to proceed if the way is clear, there is no need to wait for the green light.

Pelican Crossing - Traffic Light
Controlled

Zebra Crossing - Flashing Beacons
and 'Zebra' Stripes

A Puffin (**P**edestrian **U**ser-**F**riendly **IN**telligent) crossing is a more modern version of a pelican crossing. It has infra-red sensors which tell it if a pedestrian is actually waiting or still crossing. This allegedly cuts down on false alarms and cuts out the 'hurry up' signal allowing slower pedestrians to clear the road in their own time.

A Toucan crossing can be found where a cycle track crosses a road. It is the only crossing that cyclists can legally ride their bikes across. Because **TWO CAN** use the crossing, pedestrians and cyclists, some bright spark came up with the name!

A Pegasus crossing (I prefer that name to *'equestrian'*) is similar to a toucan crossing but can be found where a horse trail crosses a road. The wait button is situated higher up the pole for ease of access when on horseback. Both the Toucan and Pegasus crossings have infra-red sensors like the Puffin crossings.

Traffic light controlled crossings should be approached like any other set of traffic lights, but Zebra crossings should be deal with like this:

Mirror	Check behind for following vehicles.
Speed	Ease off to give more thinking time.
Look	Check for pedestrians on the pavements, they may wish to cross.
Assess	whether or not it is clear to proceed.
Decide	to proceed or give way.
Action	Stop if necessary to wait patiently. Change gear if necessary. Proceed with care when safe. DO NOT wave pedestrians across the crossing. It is their choice and they have a better view of the road. Be patient!

3) Bend / Curve:

Mirror   Check behind for following vehicles. If you can't see what's in front, then check what's behind.

Speed   Ease off to give more thinking time.

Look   Get the best view you can of the bend / curve, look well ahead.

Assess   Work out the sharpness of the bend/curve, is there a camber, is the road wet, etc.

Decide   Choose the safest speed and line for the bend / curve.

Action   Slow down and change gear if necessary, too slow is safer than too fast! Match the gear to the new speed. Be sure to use the accelerator gently as you drive round the bend / curve, this maintains traction through the corner.

4) Bus pulls over:

Mirror   Check behind for following vehicles.

Speed   Ease off to give more thinking time.

Look   Look well ahead past the bus and also at the indicators of the bus.

Assess   Is the bus stopping for long enough? Is it necessary to overtake yet? Is the road clear from oncoming traffic?

Decide   Choose to overtake or hold well back and wait.

Action   Signal before overtaking, possible gear change. If waiting, stay well back, you may need to change your mind if the bus gets delayed. Proceed with care when safe.

Naturally there are hundreds of different examples of hazards I could trawl through, but hopefully you can see that the basic approach is the same, regardless of the actual danger.

If you keep your eyes open you should see a hazard to deal with along virtually EVERY stretch of road in the Country. That should keep you on your toes.

Lesson 6: Dual-Carriageways

One more major hurdle to go! Want to go faster? Now you get the chance to stretch your legs a little and experience roads with speed limits of up to 70mph (..that's the national speed limit on a dual-carriageway in case you didn't know!).

A dual-carriageway is often a wider road that is separated by a central reservation. There may be several lanes in each direction and a higher maximum speed limit - 70mph national speed limit where permitted.

Many of the junctions to be found on dual-carriageways are identical to those all ready explained. For example, a left turn is the same no matter how many lanes are available, simply follow the routines for left emerge and enter. Hazard awareness will be just as important, but the routine will be unchanged.

Some of the other junctions do have variations when dealing with these bigger road systems. The main differences are highlighted in this section. You will find that in most cases the actual approach routine has not changed, but the action needed to complete the junction may be a little more complex.

The first important point to make about dual-carriageways is that, there is not a slow lane and a fast lane as most drivers believe. In fact the speed limit is the same in both lanes.

The left lane is the normal driving lane, and the right lane is for overtaking or using when the left lane is blocked. The right lane is also the correct position for right turns off the carriageway as I will explain shortly.

It is very important that any learner driver knows the correct position or lane to be driving in. On test, the learner must not obstruct other vehicles by being in an inappropriate lane, or inconvenience others by sudden or late lane changes.

If you know where you need to go, and the lane you need to be in, get into position early and prepare for your next move.

The Lane Change Routine

Moving from Left to Right:-	**Moving back to the Left:-**
Mirrors - Rear-view and right door mirrors.	**Mirrors** - Rear-view and left door mirrors.
Signal - Right indicator in good time.	**Signal** - Left indicator if necessary.
Position - Change lanes when clear.	**Position** - Change lanes when clear.

NOTE: Left signals when returning to the left-hand lane can sometimes be misleading to other drivers who may think you're turning or parking. Unless you are moving back in front of another driver, a left signal is unnecessary.

Dual-Carriageway - Right Emerge

Emerging onto a dual-carriageway is no more difficult than emerging from a simple T-junction. In fact, in basic terms you are just approaching a give-way line.

The difference begins once you arrive. How should you cross the carriageway safely? You want to be positive but not reckless, cautious but not hesitant. Hard questions to answer but it does get easier with practice.

Use the following routine to set you on the right track.

1) Mirrors   Rear-view and right door mirror.

2) Signal   Use the right indicator in good time

3) Position   Move to the right of your lane, towards but not over the centre line.

4) Speed   Reduce speed to stop at the give-way line. It would be highly unlikely that you could carry on without stopping. But not impossible!

5) Look   Look to see if the central reservation is wide enough for your car to wait in at the half way point. If it is, you can tackle each carriageway separately. If there is no room in the centre, it will be necessary to cross both carriageways in one movement. You must be absolutely sure the way is clear.

6) Gear   Prepare 1st gear as you approach the give-way line, you will need it. Apply the hand-brake if you are going to be waiting.

If enough room is in the centre you can drive slowly across the first carriageway, when clear from the right, to position in the central reservation. When traffic clears from the left; drive across the second carriageway to the left-hand lane to complete the junction.

If only a narrow central reservation is in place, you will need to check for traffic from both directions. When both carriageways are traffic free; drive through the central reservation curving directly into the left-hand lane. Be aware that traffic may be travelling quite fast, take great care.

Be sure to recheck the rear-view mirror as soon as you have straightened up in the new road. NEW ROAD, NEW MIRROR.

Dual-Carriageway - Right Enter

This junction involves turning off the dual-carriageway into a side-road on the right. To get to the side-road, you need to cross the right carriageway via the central reservation. In some cases a special lane will be marked out for just this purpose, but in other cases you will have to decide on the best approach position for yourself.

In either case, the first routine to follow will be the lane change. You should change into the right hand lane as soon as it is safe to do so, early positioning lets other road users know what you intend to do.

This routine is very similar to a basic right enter routine. Only the size of the road and the speed of the traffic will be different. Use the Lane Change Routine first, then:-

1) Mirrors   Rear view and right door mirror.

2) Signal   Use the right indicator in good time

3) Position   Drive in the right-hand lane up to the central reservation, then angle the car slightly to the right to give a better view of the oncoming traffic. This position also makes clear your intention to turn.

4) Speed   Use the dividing line in the central reservation as a give-way line and aim to stop at that point. It may be possible to continue in 2nd gear without stopping, but I don't recommend this for a driving test unless you are 100% sure that the road is clear.

5) Look   Look well ahead on the opposite carriageway to see any oncoming vehicles, also check the side road to be sure it is clear. Assess the situation and make your decision.

Remember, the cars may be travelling faster on this road. IF IN DOUBT, HANG ABOUT!

6) Gear   Prepare 1st gear as you position in the central reservation. If the way is clear you may proceed with care. If the carriageway is busy, wait patiently with your right signal flashing as a warning to vehicles behind. When the way is clear, proceed with care.

Be sure to recheck the rear-view mirror as soon as you have straightened up in the new road. NEW ROAD, NEW MIRROR.

Dual-Carriageway - Traffic Lights

Traffic light junctions on dual-carriageways can be enormous, seemingly hundreds of lanes, and everybody but you knows where they are going. Use **Golden Rule #1: Don't Panic!**

Where multiple lanes are involved (and they will be), make sure you get into the lane you need early and stay there. An easy rule to follow is this - Use the farthest left lane for the direction you need.

For example, if there are several lanes marked up for turning right, drive in the one that is farthest to the left. In doing so, you will be well placed in the new road, on the left-hand side or in the left-hand lane.

1) Mirrors   Rear view mirror and the corresponding door mirror for the direction you want.

2) Signal   Left for left - Right for right - No signal for ahead.

3) Position   Change into a lane marked for your direction. This should be done as soon as is safe.

4) Speed   Ease off. Be prepared to stop if the lights are red. If you are turning, reduce speed to about 15mph.

5) Look   Keep an eye on the lights as you approach. Be prepared to stop if the lights are red, but if you get to within two car lengths of the junction and the light is green, carry on. This is known as 'The Point Of No Return.'

6) Gear   a) When going Ahead - If you can simply carry on then match the gear to your current speed and re-apply the accelerator.

b) When Turning - If clear, change to 2nd gear. Proceed with care at about 15mph.

c) If you have needed to stop, prepare 1st gear ready for the next green light. Apply the hand-brake whilst waiting at the lights. If you are waiting in a queue, make sure you can see the back tyres of the car in front. Tyres On Tarmac.

When you have been waiting in the centre to turn right, don't be alarmed by the possible volume of traffic, or the amount of time you seem to have been waiting. You will get your chance to move soon, focus yourself and get ready to pull away.

Above all, use **Golden Rule #3: Take Your Time.**

Dual-Carriageway - Roundabouts

These large and often busy roundabouts are the most feared amongst my own pupils. The number of lanes and volume of traffic can easily upset a novice. But once a few have been dealt with using the same basic routines, they soon realise that bigger roundabouts can be easier to negotiate that smaller ones.

The greatest benefit is the extra space; it can be possible to assess the roundabout from 50 metres away, or more. This in turn allows for a higher speed around the roundabout (if clear). With the decisions coming sooner and usually being more obvious, dual-carriageway roundabouts are soon considered easy, and are rarely the cause of failure on test.

1) Mirrors   Rear view and left door mirror.

2) Signal   Indicate for the direction you need.

3) Position   Move into the required lane early. Normally - Left for left and ahead, Right for right. Look for road markings that may be different.

4) Speed   Slow down to about 25mph; slightly faster than other roundabouts. The larger size means that a higher speed can be maintained if the way is clear.

5) Look
Look to the right as you approach, you are looking for a space to merge into. If you see a car approaching, assess the size of the space behind, you may be able to follow it. Look for a reason to keep moving, not a reason to stop.

Remember - IF IN DOUBT, HANG ABOUT!

6) Gear
a) If you decide to go, change to 3rd gear some 30 metres or so before the junction. Drive smoothly onto the roundabout at around 20mph.

b) You may decide to slow down to 15mph or so, and then continue. This is acceptable, but you will now need 2nd gear. As you travel around the roundabout it may be possible to change back to 3rd before the exit.

c) On a busy roundabout you may still have to wait. Prepare 1st gear as you approach the line. Lift the clutch carefully to drive on or, if necessary, stop and apply the hand-brake. Proceed when clear. Be sure to change up your gears as you travel around the roundabout.

Positioning on the Roundabout

As you move around the roundabout it is important to stay to your lane, or relative position where no lanes are marked.

To Turn Left

Approach in the left lane with a left signal. Stay to the left on the roundabout and take the first exit.

To Follow the Road Ahead

Start in the left lane, drive around the outer edge of the roundabout staying in the left lane. Be sure to check the mirrors (rear and left door) and signal clearly before taking the exit.

Where the road markings have guided you into the centre or right lane to travel ahead, remain in that same relative position on the roundabout until the exit before the one you want. Check the mirrors, signal clearly, then spiral out and take the next exit.

To Turn Right

For a right turn; approach in the right-hand lane unless other lanes are marked. Remain on the inner edge of the roundabout until the exit before the one you want, Check your mirrors (rear and left door), signal clearly to the left and carefully spiral out to the left to take the next exit.

Once in the new road, as always remember to check your mirrors. New Road, New Mirror.

Dual-Carriageway - Slip Roads

Of all the junctions, the slip road is the odd one out. All other junctions follow a routine where slowing down plays a prominent role; on a slip road this could be dangerous. Slowing down is only used as a last resort when the road becomes very congested.

The most important factors to remember for slip roads are:-

1) Keep an even speed near to the speed limit.

2) Early and clear observation into the new road. Use the mirrors for this; do not look over your shoulder whilst travelling at speed.

3) Steady steering. The car should drift into the new road as for a lane change, do not swerve as this can be particularly dangerous at speed.

Follow this routine to make sure:-

1) Mirrors   Rear view and Right door mirror.

2) Signal   Indicate right in good time.

3) Position   Drift towards the right-hand side of the slip road, do not cross any hatch markings.

4) Speed   Maintain or increase the speed to match that of the cars on the carriageway.

5) Look   Take a good look in the right door mirror and a glance to the right out of the door window. You are looking for a space to drift into. Identical to a lane change.

6) Gear   a) If all is clear, no gear change is necessary. Merge across onto the carriageway.

b) If a lot of traffic is present, alter your speed to match the general flow. Change gear to match this new speed if necessary.

Once on the carriageway, check the mirror as normal and then increase speed to match traffic flow - not exceeding the limit of course.

The Manoeuvres

This is the part of the driving test in which you demonstrate your control of the vehicle to the examiner. Naturally, there is some benefit in practicing sharp steering and reversing, as these skills will come in very handy in real life. But for now, you should focus on the fact that this is not yet real life driving, this is your driving test.

The examiner does not want to see how fast you can make the car twist and turn, or how efficiently you can get from A to B. The examiner wants to see three skills being demonstrated; all three skills. Only two out of three will surely result in a fail. The three skills are given a name, I call them **CORA**.

Control of the car. Generally control of speed by correct use of the foot pedals. You must be able to maintain a steady, slow speed throughout. The car should not struggle or stall, nor should it speed out of control.

Observation. To have complete awareness of the surroundings, of vehicles and pedestrians, and react correctly to them. Waiting for the road to be clear, and remain clear, may take some time - so be it.

Reasonable **A**ccuracy. To be able to perform the manoeuvre as it should be, without losing position, endangering yourself or others. Do not hit the kerbs. Certain leeway is given, hence the word 'reasonable'.

When all three of these skills are shown together, the examiner would simply move to the next part of the test - job done.

There are more manoeuvres allowed on the test than most people realise. You have, in total, SEVEN manoeuvres to cover... although most Driving Instructors (including myself) will only teach six of them - The reverse around a right-hand corner although still on the official syllabus is NOT* used on test (*at least I've not seen it used and I've been teaching since 1996!).

So the SIX manoeuvres you need to know are:

The Turn in the Road - Commonly called a three-point-turn, but could be completed as a five-point-turn as long as it was in control. Here's where you will gain real skill with Clutch Control and Steering Coordination.

Reverse around a Left-Hand Corner - They rarely (if ever) go to the right, but often choose this 'unpopular' manoeuvre. It really isn't as hard as people think in fact once I show you how it's done, you'll wonder what all the fuss was about!

Reverse Park on the Road - Usually called the parallel park. This is the one where you reverse into a gap between two parked cars at the side of the road. Just follow the simple steps I'll give you and this one is a piece of cake.

Reverse Park in a Car Park (Left) - Usually called the bay park. This manoeuvre will ONLY be done in the Driving Test Centre Car Park.

Reverse Park in a Car Park (Right) - The choice of left or right bay park will normally be YOUR choice. However, if there are no available spaces on your preferred side... you will have to go the other way. I'll make sure you are happy either way... then it really won't matter.

The Emergency Stop - The final manoeuvre is requested at random by the Driving Examiner. You might have to do this, you might not. But if you do, you will still have to perform one of the other manoeuvres.

Since the introduction of ABS (Anti-Lock Braking Systems) in cars as standard on most models, the skill of stopping without skidding is no longer required. Simply stamping on the brake pedal could still stop the car safely, so there's not very much for the examiners to test any more. As a result, the emergency stop is no longer classed as a manoeuvre and is gradually being phased out.

In light of that fact, I won't be covering the emergency stop in this book. I'll leave that to your instructor.

The following chapters concentrate on the basic four manoeuvres, five if you count bay parking both ways, but as a final word of encouragement:

Don't worry, you will only be asked to perform ONE of the manoeuvres on the test.

The catch is that you won't know which one until you're doing it!

Learn them all and that won't matter.

PLEASE NOTE:

Videos of all the lessons, with full talk through, are available at www.VirtualDrivingSchool.co.uk

Use coupon code **HTPYDT** to get **20% OFF**

Lesson 7: The Turn In The Road

This manoeuvre is often referred to as the 3-point-turn, but it's correct and full title is "the turn in the road using forward and reverse gears". In theory a 5-point-turn would be acceptable if it were performed under full control with sufficient observation.

Throughout the exercise you must demonstrate **CORA** in order to achieve the correct standard for the driving test.

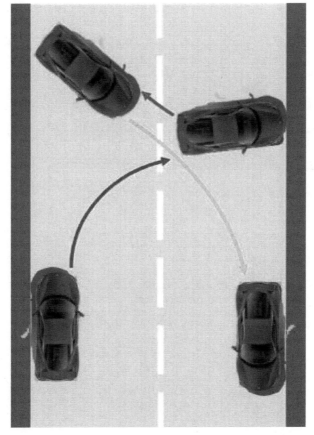

Follow these simple steps to fit the manoeuvre together:-

Stage #1 – Forwards

1) Select 1st gear and use full observation to be sure the road is clear before beginning. Check out of every window; front, side and back.

2) Gentle clutch control gets the car in motion. If your clutch comes too high your car will move too fast.

3) Turn the steering wheel full-lock to the RIGHT, as quickly as possible without crossing your hands. The car should only have moved about a metre so far.

4) Observation again, look left and right as you cross the road. At this point if you saw a vehicle approaching, you should continue. The vehicle will have an opportunity to pass you shortly. Do not rush to move out of their way.

5) Balance the clutch to maintain a slow, steady movement across the road. Be aware that the response may alter with the camber of the road, depending on whether you are driving up-hill or down-hill.

6) As you approach the far kerb, straighten the wheels. Again be sure to <u>not</u> cross your hands. Remember - if you need one and a half turns to get to full-lock, you need one and a half turns to straighten up again!

7)   Push the clutch to the floor and then gently brake to stop the car. You should be just short of the kerb, do not be overhanging or touching the kerb.

8)   Secure the car - handbrake and neutral.

Stage #2 - Reversing

1)   Select reverse gear and use full observation to be sure the road is once again clear. If vehicles are approaching, wait patiently. Drivers sometimes stop and wait for learners to finish this manoeuvre, if this is the case just continue. Do not rush. The driver has chosen to wait, you did not force them, and they could have passed if they had wanted.

2)   Gentle clutch control combined with a hill start, gets the car in motion. A hill start is usually required due to the camber of the road.

3)   Turn the steering wheel full-lock to the LEFT.

4)   Take another look left and right before focusing your attention out of the rear window.

5)   Balance the clutch for slow, steady movement across the road.

6)   As you approach the kerb, straighten the wheels.

7)   Push the clutch to the floor and gently brake to stop.

8)   Secure the car - handbrake and neutral.

Stage #3 - Forwards

1)   Select 1st gear and use full observation. Again if there are vehicles approaching, wait patiently.

2)   Gentle clutch control combined with a hill start, gets the car in motion.

3)   Turn the steering wheel to the RIGHT, as much as is needed to gain normal road position. This may or may not be full-lock.

4)   Take another look to the left and right.

5)   Balance the clutch for slow and steady movement.

6)   When the car is straight, straighten the wheels.

7)   Check the mirrors - rear view and door mirrors - before accelerating.

When the exercise is over, go back to your basic driving routines, you have not finished the test yet!

Lesson 8: Reverse into a Side-Road

I am constantly amazed by the amount of pupils I get who claim they can't reverse. They turn the wrong way because 'the steering is backwards', or they have no idea where the car is in relation to the kerb. I sit patiently and listen to all the excuses before showing them how to do it simply and effectively, using a routine.

This routine does need to be modified for each corner as each corner is going to be different; sharper, shallower, more up-hill, more down-hill. All corners vary, but your approach to this manoeuvre should be consistent. Certain aspects will always look the same, regardless of the type of corner.

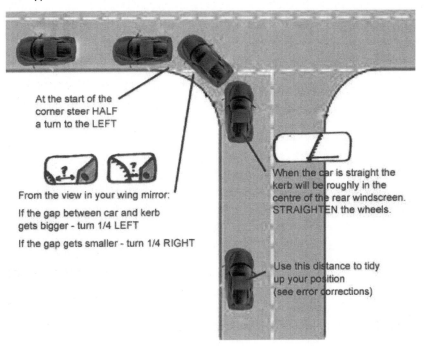

At the start of the corner steer HALF a turn to the LEFT

From the view in your wing mirror:

If the gap between car and kerb gets bigger - turn 1/4 LEFT

If the gap gets smaller - turn 1/4 RIGHT

When the car is straight the kerb will be roughly in the centre of the rear windscreen. STRAIGHTEN the wheels.

Use this distance to tidy up your position (see error corrections)

Follow this routine; you'll soon get the hang of it.

The Approach:

1)   Drive past the side road and position your car about 2ft away from the kerb, and about a car length past the corner. You should be far enough past when you can see the corner in the rear view mirror. Stop and secure the car at this position.

2)   Select reverse gear and use full observation. The road and pavements should be clear before you begin, if they are not then wait patiently.

3)   Gentle clutch control gets the car in motion.

4)   Observation. You should have a continuous check for traffic approaching from all directions and also watch for the first and crucial turning point.

5)   The first turning point is as the back of the car gets to the beginning of the corner.

NOTE: There will be a variety of ways to identify this point. The one I teach is to make use of the left door mirror. If the mirror is angled slightly downward so as to be able to see the rear wheel arch and the kerb, it is possible to see when the rear wheel gets to the point of turn. This is accurate for all types of corner regardless of sharpness.

Other methods, such as using matchsticks in the rear window, will only be effective on certain corners in that car. This method works all the time in whatever vehicle you are driving.

The Corner:

1)   Look around to be sure the way is clear. It is especially important to check your blind spot over your right shoulder.

2)   Turn the steering wheel a half turn to the left. This will probably not be enough to get the car all the way around the corner, but it will get things moving in the right direction.

3)   Balance the clutch to give slow and steady movement.

4)   Watch the line of the kerb for any sideways movement. The best places to look are out of the rear window and the rear right window. From there you can get the big picture and see the new road that you are aiming for. It is also possible to use the right door mirror, but overuse of this mirror should be avoided.

5)   If and when the car begins to drift away from the kerb, you should add extra steering in small amounts.

NOTE: Add a quarter of a turn to the left and see how the car reacts, if you are still drifting away then add another quarter turn. It is always best to under-steer and then add extra when it is needed, if you were to do too much steering at the beginning you would hit the kerb, and that would be very difficult to correct.

6)   Observation. Every few seconds you should take the time to look around, if a vehicle approaches from any direction, stop and wait patiently.

7)   Keep moving slowly around the corner. A little over two thirds of the way around the corner, you will see the straight kerb in the rear window. This is the kerb-line for the new road. You are well on course but do not yet straighten the wheels.

8)   When the new kerb-line appears to be in the centre of your rear window, the car will be in a straight line with the new road. This position can be checked by looking in the left door mirror; you should see the kerb-line parallel to the car. At this point you must straighten the wheels quickly.

Straightening Up:

Having straightened the wheels, you must make sure the car is in the correct position.

You should be straight and about 2ft or less from the kerb. If this is the case then you simply reverse until invited to stop by the examiner. If not, then you must fix the situation before stopping.

If your car is not in the correct position, it will be in one of the following positions.

Error #1:- The car is drifting away from the kerb.

This suggests that you have straightened the wheels a little early and the car has not yet finished the corner. A simple correction in steering is needed.

Solution:-

1)   Make a quarter turn to the LEFT. Hold until the car is perfectly straight, and then...

2)   Straighten the wheels. Continue to reverse until invited to stop.

Error #2:- The car is drifting toward the kerb.

This suggests that you were a little slow to straighten the wheels. The car has travelled too far around the corner and could be in danger of hitting the kerb. Again, only a simple correction is needed.

Solution:-

1)   Make a quarter turn to the RIGHT. Hold until the car is perfectly straight, and then...

2)   Straighten the wheels and continue to reverse.

Error #3:- The car is straight but is too far from the kerb.

This is caused by under-steering as you turned the corner, which allowed the car to drift wide. This can still be fixed so long as you have not strayed so wide as to be unreasonably accurate. That will be a judgment call for the examiner on the day.

Solution:-

1)   Make a quarter turn to the LEFT. Allow the car to drift towards the kerb, check the left door mirror for accuracy.

2)   When you're close enough to the kerb, straighten the wheels and then make a quarter turn to the RIGHT. Allow the car to become straight

3)   Straighten the wheels when the car is straight and continue to reverse for about two car lengths or until invited to stop.

Remember - Always get the car straight first, and then straighten the wheels.

Lesson 9: Reverse Parking

The Reverse Park on the road or Parallel Park is possibly the quickest and easiest of the manoeuvres to learn.

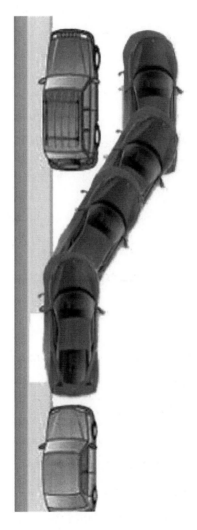

There are lots of different styles for this manoeuvre, some with turning points to aim for, some with pure judgment as the main factor and some which have to be inch perfect or you scratch the car!

I teach a 4-turning-point method, but if your way works... use it.

For the driving test, the boundaries are clear. Reasonable accuracy, which means that when finished your car should be parked no more than two car lengths behind the parked vehicle and within 2ft from the kerb. This gives you plenty of room, much more than you would have in real life outside the shops.

At this stage I want you to accept that your CONTROL is achieved with gentle movement of the clutch, and that your OBSERVATION will be continuous throughout the manoeuvre. Should you see any other vehicle approaching, stop and wait patiently.

However, it is worth pointing out that an observation check to your blind spot over your right shoulder should be made prior to the first turning point. Check the road is clear before you swing out!

As for the REASONABLE ACCURACY... Follow these steps:-

1) Position your car along side and about 2ft away from the target vehicle. Make sure your car and wheels are straight at this point.

2) **The 1st Turning Point.** Line up your left door mirror about half way along the parked car. Turn the wheels full-lock to the LEFT.

3) **The 2nd Turning Point.** Allow the car to swing out towards a 45° angle, diagonally across the road. This is a maximum angle, do not swing out further. STRAIGHTEN the wheels.

4) **The 3rd Turning Point.** Allow the car to slowly roll backwards until the rear of the car is about 2 to 3 feet from the kerb. Check the left door mirror to see the position. Turn full-lock to the RIGHT.

5)   **The 4th Turning Point.** Allow the front of the car to swing in until the car is parallel to the kerb. STRAIGHTEN the wheels.

6)   As soon as the car and the wheels are straight, STOP and secure.

If you have followed these turning points then the manoeuvre has worked. Combine this accuracy with FULL observation and control, and it will be satisfactory on test.

Lesson 10: Bay Parking

In areas where the driving test centre has use of its own car park, it is likely that the bay park manoeuvre will be used to replace the parallel park. Quite simply, the manoeuvre involves reversing into a parking space or bay within the car park.

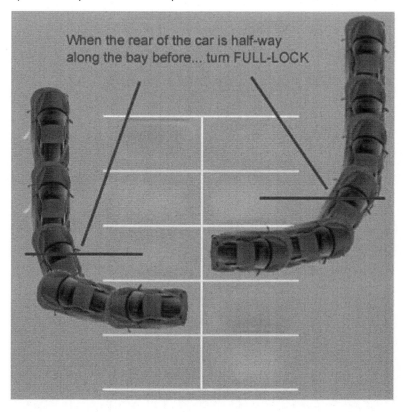

To be considered reasonably accurate, the car must be positioned between the bay lines, far enough back so the front of the car does not stick out of the bay, but not back far enough to stick out of the back of the bay. The car does not have to be perfectly straight, although it looks better if it is, but all four wheels must be within the bay. If a wheel is on the line, it is considered to be in. Over the line and it's considered out.

Follow this simple routine to get this manoeuvre to work, but be prepared for some trial and error. It may take a few goes before you perfect your aim.

1)   Position your car at right angles to the bays about 1.5 to 2 metres away from the front line. Further if you have the space. Make sure that you allow some room for the car to swing out, don't go too close to a wall or other parked cars.

2)   Carefully check all around before beginning the manoeuvre. As with all the manoeuvres, observation is critical. You are looking for other vehicles and pedestrians in the car park.

3)   Choose a bay some distance behind the car to aim for and slowly reverse in a straight line towards it. You begin your turn as the back of your car reaches about half way across the bay before the one you are aiming for. This is where your judgement and a little practice come in.

4)   After another look around the car park, turn the wheels to full-lock. This can be either left or right depending on the position of the bay. Continue to look around as the front of

the car swings out.

5)   When the car straightens up in line with the bay, straighten the wheels and reverse into the bay. Come back far enough to be fully inside the marked bay.

6)   Stop and secure the car.

Of course it is highly possible that you may miss the bay using this method, until you have practiced your aim. But there are a couple of tips I can give to help you correct your accuracy on the move.

As you pass the 45 degree point, i.e. half way towards the bay, make use of your left door mirror. If it is angled down sufficiently, you will be able to see the bay line coming into view.

Problem #1:

When reversing to the LEFT: If the line seems a little far away from the left side of the car, it suggests that you may have started turning too late.

At that point you can stop and move forwards turning to the right. This will narrow the angle and line you up with the bay behind. When you are happy that your car is in line, reverse into the bay.

Problem #2:

However, if the line seems too close to the side of the car, perhaps disappearing beneath the car, then it suggests that you started to turn too early.

This correction is a little simpler. Straighten out the wheels to widen your curve, just as you would to move wider from the kerb on the reverse around a corner. As the gap between the car and the line widens (viewed in the left door mirror), turn back to full lock and continue the turn into the bay.

If you are reversing to the right then a mirror image of these corrections would be needed. But don't be afraid to pull out and have another go. Fix it and finish it!

On test you are allowed to make a correction, but I would suggest that you make it count. Reposition once if you need to, but don't drift out of position again. You may not be allowed a second shuffle.

If a correction is needed, be sure to make it a timely correction. If you reverse more than half way into the parking bay, the examiner may not allow you to shuffle forwards. The problem should have been seen and dealt with earlier than that.

As you play around with this manoeuvre, you will learn a great deal about how your car turns and what it's capable of. Don't be put off by the presence of other parked cars in the car park. It is actually easier to park next to another car than to park in the open. The simple reason for this is that you can use the other car as a marker. If you park a couple of feet away from it, you are sure to be within the bay.

Good luck. Keep practicing.

In Conclusion

You're nearly there now... just one more road type to cover. Here's your chance to have some fun on my personal favourite - The Country Road. There are plenty of national speed limit (60mph) country roads around... some straight... some curvy... some wide... and some very narrow.

During this time you will get a real feel for Speed Control and ability to Read the Road Ahead. One of the most important lessons to learn here is how to switch from 'faster' roads to 'slower' roads so you can maintain a SAFE speed at all times.

Are you READY to take a driving test?

Let's find out. Get your Driving Instructor to take you up to the Driving Test Centre and put you through a 'Mock Test'. He'll make it as realistic as possible - just giving directions, no instruction - and possibly even go around one of the Official Driving Test Routes. Your instructor will mark you just as the Driving Test Examiner would and you'll find out if you are ready to PASS.

Practice. Practice. Practice...

These are the three most important words. The Mock Test has 'probably' shown up your weaknesses, so it's time to put it right.

When you can complete a route without making 'silly' mistakes then... You Are Ready To Go For Your Driving Test... For Real.

Please be aware that the average learner driver WILL NOT learn all this in 10 HOURS. You should work through the 10 lessons at your own pace. Some lessons will take less than an hour but others may take 3 or 4 hours practice to master. Your Driving Instructor SHOULD NOT hold you back, but neither should they push you if you're not ready.

Most of my pupils reach the high standard required in around 30 to 40 hours but, as you are an individual, I can't say how many you will personally need to reach that level, it will naturally depend on your own ability and willingness to learn.

As a final word... May I wish you the very best of luck if you have your driving test soon. Please let me know how you get on.

Oh yes... **Golden Rule #2:**

Everyone else on the road... is an IDIOT!

Safe driving.

Phill Godridge BSc DSA ADI

FINAL NOTE:

Videos of all the lessons, with full talk through, are available at www.VirtualDrivingSchool.co.uk

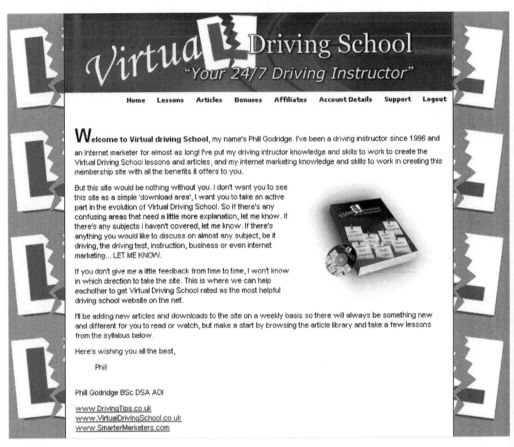

Use coupon code **HTPYDT** to get **20% OFF**

Printed in Great Britain
by Amazon.co.uk, Ltd.,
Marston Gate.